Instant Windows PowerShell 3.0 Windows Management Instrumentation Starter

Explore new abilities of Powershell 3.0 to interact with Windows Management Instrumentation (WMI) through the use of the new CIM cmdlets and realistic management scenarios

Brenton J.W. Blawat

BIRMINGHAM - MUMBAI

Instant Windows PowerShell 3.0 Windows Management Instrumentation Starter

First published: March 2013

Production Reference: 1200313

Published by Packt Publishing Ltd.
Livery Place
35 Livery Street
Birmingham B3 2PB, UK.

ISBN 978-1-84968-962-5

www.packtpub.com

Credits

Author

Brenton J.W. Blawat

Reviewer

TJ McAteer

Acquisition Editor

Akram Hussain

Commissioning Editor

Harsha Bharwani

Technical Editor

Dominic Pereira

Copy Editor

Ruta Waghmare

Project Coordinator

Esha Thakker

Proofreader

Aaron Nash

Graphics

Aditi Gajjar

Production Coordinator

Melwyn D'sa

Cover Work

Melwyn D'sa

Cover Image

Manu Joseph

About the Author

Brenton J.W. Blawat is an Author, Entrepreneur, Strategic Technical Advisor, and Engineer who has a passion for the procurement of technology in organizations. He is business-centric, while technology minded, and has many years of experience bridging the gap between the technical staff and decision makers in organizations. Brenton prides himself in his ability to effectively communicate to a diverse audience and provide strategic direction for small and large organizations alike. Throughout his career, he has worked for a multitude of Fortune 500 organizations, and specializes in delivery automation and workflow optimizations.

I dedicate all the contributions made by me in this book to my father, William Michael Blawat, "Byśmy zawsze pamiętali". I would like to thank Curtis John for being a mentor, role model, and friend. I attribute my successes in life to these two individuals.

About the Reviewer

Thomas "TJ" McAteer is an engineer specializing in complex Microsoft implementations and special projects. He has worked for several years in the industry, specializing in backup and disaster recovery, as well as network design and active directory/exchange architecture and implementation. He holds current certification in Microsoft, Cisco, and VMware technologies.

When not working, TJ spends time with his new wife Kaitlyn and attempts to feed his addiction to snowboarding. He currently works at Atomic Data on the Microsoft Implementation team. Atomic Data is an IT-services provider, headquartered in Minneapolis, Minnesota. With data centers in diverse locations across the globe and a highly skilled team of engineers, developers, and customer service representatives, Atomic is a one-stop shop. Atomic Data can build a solution for everything from a client's first website, to virtual server infrastructure, cloud computing, and enterprise architecture consulting. Atomic provides clients with engineering know how, lightning-fast response times, and customizable and flexible levels of service. Combined with a 24 x 7 x 365 Network Operations Center and Service Desk, Atomic Data has simple, safe, and smart technology solutions to solve nearly any business problem.

"If I have seen further, it is by standing on the shoulders of giants" – Sir Isaac Newton

I would like to take this opportunity to thank Ryan Bloch and Jim Wolford. Without their support and backing I would not be the engineer I am today. It is also important to thank Brenton Blawat as without him none of this would be possible.

www.packtpub.com

Support files, eBooks, discount offers and more

You might want to visit www.packtpub.com for support files and downloads related to your book.

Did you know that Packt offers eBook versions of every book published, with PDF and ePub files available? You can upgrade to the eBook version at www.packtpub.com and as a print book customer, you are entitled to a discount on the eBook copy. Get in touch with us at service@packtpub.com for more details.

At www.packtpub.com, you can also read a collection of free technical articles, sign up for a range of free newsletters and receive exclusive discounts and offers on Packt books and eBooks.

packtLib.packtpub.com

Do you need instant solutions to your IT questions? PacktLib is Packt's online digital book library. Here, you can access, read and search across Packt's entire library of books.

Why Subscribe?

- Fully searchable across every book published by Packt
- Copy and paste, print and bookmark content
- On demand and accessible via web browser

Free Access for Packt account holders

If you have an account with Packt at www.packtpub.com, you can use this to access PacktLib today and view nine entirely free books. Simply use your login credentials for immediate access.

Table of Contents

Instant Windows PowerShell 3.0 Windows Management Instrumentation Starter

Welcome to the *Instant Windows PowerShell 3.0 Windows Management Instrumentation Starter*. This book has been created to provide you with the necessary tools to develop in PowerShell 3.0 and create scripts to successfully manage desktop and server environments. Through leveraging Windows Management Instrumentation (WMI), you will be able to create scripts for a structured deployment of software, systems management, and system health checks.

This book contains the following sections:

So, what is PowerShell 3.0 WMI? – learn what Windows Management Instrumentation (WMI) is, how PowerShell 3.0 utilizes it, and why it's applicable to systems engineers.

Installation – learn how to download and install PowerShell 3.0 with ease and verify if the correct version is installed on a system.

Quick start – this section guides you on how to perform basic WMI queries utilizing PowerShell 3.0, including the new PowerShell cmdlets.

Top features you need to know about – this section provides three scenarios leveraging Windows Management Instrumentation (WMI) and PowerShell 3.0. By the end of this section you will be able to deploy software, dynamically provision systems, and perform system maintenance using PowerShell 3.0.

People and places you should get to know – PowerShell 3.0 has a strong community of professionals that provide support for beginner and advanced users. This section gives additional resources for reference that provide PowerShell 3.0 examples, detailed articles, blogs, and links to members in the PowerShell community.

So, what is PowerShell 3.0 WMI?

Microsoft created **Windows Management Instrumentation** (**WMI**) as a management layer to the Windows operating system. This management layer allows you to retrieve information pertaining to the operating system or physical hardware on a system. It also allows you to manipulate components within the operating system.

A good example for this section is a hard drive. WMI provides the ability to view the physical hard drive as well as the logical components of the hard drive. Using a call to the `Win32_diskdrive` class, you have the ability to view the physical aspects of the disk drive, such as the tracks, sectors, manufacturer, and even the serial number. The `win32_logicaldisk` class provides you with the ability to see the logical aspects of a drive, such as partitions, free space, and volume names.

Not limited to just Windows operating system management, WMI also has the extensibility to allow third-party developers to create WMI providers for use within their projects. This means that you can create the management hooks within your code that will allow remote management through a common standardized framework. Many companies have adopted the use of WMI providers for items such as storage subsystems, application virtualization, hardware virtualization, and enhanced management of the hardware connected to a workstation or server system.

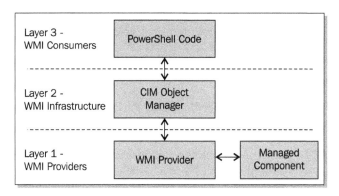

Microsoft chose to follow the **Common Information Model** (**CIM**) industry standard for WMI. The preceding diagram takes a simplified look at Microsoft's implementation of WMI through the use of the CIM standard. There are three layers to their model, which are as follows:

✦ **WMI consumers**: The WMI consumers are exactly what their name states. They consume the available APIs to access the managed component. The WMI consumers are the real users of the C/C++ and .NET clients, and they use scripting languages, such as PowerShell 3.0, to access management data and interact with the managed components. In the hard drive example, the WMI consumer is the PowerShell code that calls information about the hard drive. This would look as follows:

```
get-wmiobject -class win32_logicaldisk
```

✦ **WMI infrastructure**: The WMI infrastructure includes the **CIM Object Manager** (**CIMOM**), which stores a repository of the available WMI providers. If a third-party WMI provider doesn't register with the CIM Object Manager, the Windows operating system will not be able to manage the component through WMI. In the hard drive example, the CIMOM will import the **Managed Object Format** (**MOF**) file of the hard drive into the WMI repository. This will register the hard drive's available WMI properties and methods into use by a WMI consumer.

✦ **WMI providers**: The last components, WMI providers, are made up of a driver (DLL) and a MOF file. These two components are responsible for returning the management data to the WMI consumer, through the WMI infrastructure. This allows the WMI consumer to interact with the managed components. In the hard drive example, the WMI consumer will access the hard drive through the WMI infrastructure utilizing the hard drive driver (DLL). The WMI consumer will have the ability to retrieve the information pertaining to the physical components on that hard drive.

WMI integration with PowerShell 3.0

PowerShell has the ability to interact with WMI through the use of the built-in cmdlets. These cmdlets act as the WMI consumers and interact with the WMI. As WMI evolved with the release of new operating systems, PowerShell also needed to evolve in parallel to manage those systems. With the release of Windows 8 and Windows Server 2012, Microsoft created a new iteration of the Microsoft **Windows Management Framework** (**WMF**), Version 3.0. The new release of Windows Management Framework updates WMI to Version 3.0, PowerShell to Version 3.0, and installs the new **Windows Remote Management** (**WinRM**), **OData IIS Extensions**, and **Server Manager CIM Provider**.

PowerShell 3.0 includes new WMI management cmdlets, displayed in the following table, which leverage the use of the new functionality within Windows Management Framework 3.0. The new CIM cmdlets provide a richer WMI experience leveraging stateful communications to the remote systems. They also provide the ability to create CIM calls through PowerShell 3.0 to non-Windows-based WMI systems that support **Web Services-Management** (**WSman**). This provides engineers the ability to tap into a variety of systems for management purposes.

Get-CimAssociatedInstance	New-CimSession
Get-CimClass	New-CimSessionOption
Get-CimInstance	Register-CimIndicationEvent
Get-CimSession	Remove-CimInstance
Invoke-CimMethod	Remove-CimSession
New-CimInstance	Set-CimInstance

Using PowerShell in your environment

PowerShell is quickly becoming the de-facto standard for managing the Windows-based systems in small and large organizations. It is being used for tasks, such as automated software deployments, dynamic system provisioning, and system maintenance. It is also being heavily used in Microsoft products, such as System Center 2012 - Service Manager, that allow for business process automation.

PowerShell 3.0 has introduced a variety of new cmdlets that further simplify the administration of systems through the use of WMI. Whatever the administrative task, the PowerShell community has several examples of the ways to manage systems through the use of the WMI consumers.

The examples provided in this book are just the tip of the iceberg compared to what you can accomplish utilizing PowerShell 3.0 and Windows Management Instrumentation. You may be surprised by the number of manual administration steps that can be automated by creating PowerShell scripts. The sky is the limit when it comes to scripting with PowerShell!

Installation

PowerShell 3.0 is available for a variety of operating systems. These include Windows 7 SP1, Windows 8, Windows Server 2008 SP2, Windows Server 2008 R2 SP1, and Windows Server 2012. Microsoft made the decision to restrict the use of PowerShell 3.0 on operating systems prior to Windows 7 and Server 2008 SP2 and they are not supported by the latest release of PowerShell.

 For systems that have Windows 8 and Windows Server 2012, PowerShell 3.0 is included with the operating system, and no further installation is required.

In three easy steps, you can install PowerShell 3.0 and be ready to start leveraging the new WMI 3.0 functionality introduced with PowerShell 3.0.

1. First, you will install the .NET Framework 4.0.

2. Second, you will install Windows Management Framework 3.0.

3. Finally, you will configure the PowerShell 3.0 security setting for use on a system.

Step 1 – prerequisite software - .NET Framework 4.0

Before you install PowerShell 3.0, you will need to install the .NET Framework 4.0. The fastest way to download and install the .NET Framework is to perform the following steps:

1. Download the Microsoft .NET Framework 4.0 by browsing to `http://www.microsoft.com/en-us/download/details.aspx?id=17851`.

 Prior to downloading the Microsoft .NET Framework, you may be prompted to install Windows Internet Explorer 9 and Microsoft Windows Malicious Software Removal Tool. These are not required for the installation of PowerShell 3.0.

2.   Select **No Thanks and Continue** (optional).

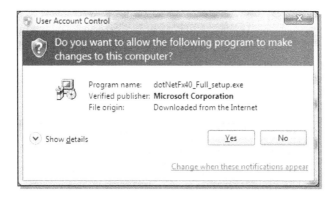

3.   When prompted to download, select **Run**.

4.   When prompted to install, select **Yes**.

5.   Select **I have Read and I Accept the License Terms**.

6.   Select **Install**.

7.   Select **Finish**.

8.   After the installation, you should restart the computer.

Step 2 – installing the Windows Management Framework 3.0

The Windows Management Framework 3.0 consists of updates to a variety of components. Most notably, the updates include PowerShell 3.0, Windows Remote Management, and Windows Management Instrumentation 3.0. To ease the installation of each of these components, Microsoft chose to bundle them into a single installer package.

The fastest way to download and install the Windows Management Framework 3.0 is to perform the following steps:

1. Download the Windows Management Framework 3.0 by browsing to `http://www.microsoft.com/en-us/download/details.aspx?id=34595`.

2. For Windows 7 SP1, and Windows 2008 R2 SP1, download the software with the knowledge base number **KB2506143**, select **Download and Open**.

3. For Windows Server 2008 SP2, download the software with the knowledge base number **KB2506146** and select **Download and Open**.

4. When prompted to install the Windows update for the selected knowledge base number as mentioned in the preceding steps, select **Yes**.

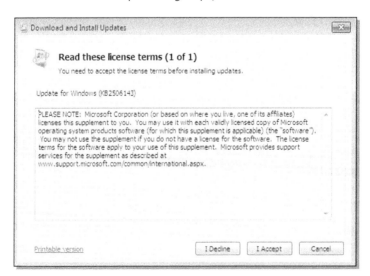

5. When prompted with a EULA, select **I Accept**.

6. When prompted after the installation, select **Restart Now**.

Step 3 – preparing to use the new CIM cmdlets

There are two methods that you can use to configure a system for use with the new CIM cmdlets. The first method, using the quick configuration, is the least secure way to configure the system. It creates blanket firewall rules that open the inbound ports 80 and 5985 (default) for HTTP and 5986 for HTTPS (default) to all systems. The second method, manual configuration, can provide a more granular approach to the configuration of a system and provides opportunities to better secure the systems. Whichever method you choose to configure Windows Remote Management, it should be performed on both the source and destination systems for the use of the CIM cmdlets.

Quick configuration

It is important to remember that if you are using web services on the systems, you are performing a quick configuration and the default configuration process opens port 80 for use with Windows Remote Management. The WinRM listener may cause conflicts with web services, and manual configuration may be the best approach.

To utilize the quick configuration option of the Windows Remote Management configuration process, perform the following steps:

1. Select **Start**. In the **Start** menu's **Search**, type `Powershell.exe`.

2. Right-click on **Powershell.exe** | **Select Run as Administrator** (this operation requires administrative privileges).

3. Type the following command to start the quick configuration process:

   `WinRm quickconfig`

4. To set the Windows Remote Management Service to Automatic (Delayed), press *Y* and press *Enter*.

5. To open the firewall for `http://*` for Window Remote Management, press *Y* and press *Enter*.

6. Windows Remote Management is now configured to start automatically and the necessary ports are open for use within the Windows Firewall.

Manual configuration of system

To get started in this section, you need to start the Windows Remote Management service. For security purposes, this service is set to a manual start by default:

Windows Presentation Foundation Font Cache 3.0....	Optimizes performan...		Manual	Local Service
Windows Remote Management (WS-Management)	Windows Remote Ma...	Started	Manual	Network S...
Windows Search	Provides content inde...	Started	Automatic (D...	Local Syste...

To start the Windows Remote Management service, perform the following steps:

1. Select **Start**. In the **Search** option, type `Services.msc`.

2. Press *Enter*. Browse to **Windows Remote Management (WS-Management)**.

3. Right-click on **Windows Remote Management (WS-Management)** and select **Start**.

WinRM relies on a trusted connection between the source and destination systems for security purposes. If you are not on a domain, or are on a non-trusted domain, you will need to add the target system as a trusted host in WinRM. This is not required on a domain, as the domain-level authentication mechanisms will provide for what are trusted and non-trusted systems.

To add a trusted host, perform the following steps:

1. Select **Start**. In the **Search** option, type `Powershell.exe`.

2. Right-click on **Powershell.exe**, and select **Run as Administrator** (this operation requires administrative privileges).

```
Administrator: Windows PowerShell
PS C:\Windows\system32> winrm get winrm/config/client
Client
    NetworkDelayms = 5000
    URLPrefix = wsman
    AllowUnencrypted = false
    Auth
        Basic = true
        Digest = true
        Kerberos = true
        Negotiate = true
        Certificate = true
        CredSSP = false
    DefaultPorts
        HTTP = 5985
        HTTPS = 5986
    TrustedHosts = packtpub

PS C:\Windows\system32>
```

 When using a command to add a trusted host, it will replace the entry of the existing trusted host systems. This will require you to take note of the existing systems that are in the trusted list, and re-add them with the new entries.

3. To list the existing trusted host systems, type the following command and press *Enter*:

```
winrm get winrm/config/client
```

```
Administrator: Windows PowerShell
PS C:\Windows\system32> Winrm set winrm/config/client '@{TrustedHosts="packtpub,packtpub1"}'
Client
    NetworkDelayms = 5000
    URLPrefix = wsman
    AllowUnencrypted = false
    Auth
        Basic = true
        Digest = true
        Kerberos = true
        Negotiate = true
        Certificate = true
        CredSSP = false
    DefaultPorts
        HTTP = 5985
        HTTPS = 5986
    TrustedHosts = packtpub,packtpub1

PS C:\Windows\system32>
```

4. To add the systems to the trusted host, type the following command and press *Enter*:

```
Winrm set winrm/config/client '@{TrustedHosts="RemoteSystemName,Ex
istingTrustedSystem"}'
```

The last part in the manual configuration of the system is to open the firewall ports for use with Windows Remote Management. By default, Win-RM uses 5985 for HTTP and 5986 for HTTPS.

1. Select **Start** and enter `Powershell.exe` in the **Search** option.

2. Right-click on **Powershell.exe**, and select **Run as Administrator** (this operation requires administrative privileges).

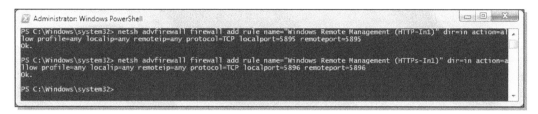

3. To open the HTTP ports using `netsh`, type the following command and press *Enter*:

    ```
    netsh advfirewall firewall add rule name="Windows Remote
    Management (HTTP-In1)" dir=in action=allow profile=any localip=any
    remoteip=any protocol=TCP localport=5895 remoteport=5895
    ```

4. Upon successful execution of the command, you will receive an `Ok.` message in the command line.

5. To open the HTTPS ports using `netsh`, type the following command and press *Enter*:

    ```
    netsh advfirewall firewall add rule name="Windows Remote
    Management (HTTPs-In1)" dir=in action=allow profile=any
    localip=any remoteip=any protocol=TCP localport=5896
    remoteport=5896
    ```

6. Upon successful execution of the command, you will receive an `Ok.` message in the command line.

For more information on the `netsh advfirewall` firewall command and ways to better secure the Windows firewall, go to `http://technet.microsoft.com/en-us/library/cc771920(v=ws.10).aspx`.

And that's it! But how do I know it's installed?

An important point to remember is that Microsoft has kept the installation path for PowerShell as `C:\Windows\System32\WindowsPowerShell\v1.0\`. This can be misleading to you as the PowerShell version changes, but the installation path version doesn't change.

The discrepancy in the installation path was done purposely for development and reverse compatibility reasons. When creating a program, a developer can add an assembly reference to `System.Management.Automation` for referencing PowerShell within the code. This assembly reference lives in the path by which PowerShell is installed. Since Microsoft doesn't allow multiple versions of PowerShell to be installed on the same computer, the applications that were developed in v1 would have to be recompiled, pointing to v2 as the installation path. Subsequently, the iterations of PowerShell would be required for those applications to be recompiled again. Instead, Microsoft kept the path of v1.0 for all the subsequent releases, thus ensuring reverse compatibility with the previous versions of the PowerShell applications.

There are three quick methods that can be performed to verify the correct version number of PowerShell 3.0. Start by opening PowerShell 3.0:

1. Select **Start**. In the **Search** option, type `PowerShell.exe`.

2. Press *Enter*.

Method 1 – Get-Host cmdlet

After starting `Powershell.exe`, perform the following steps:

1. Type `get-host`.

2. Press *Enter*.

3. You will see that the version is **3.0**:

Method 2 – looking at version table

After starting `Powershell.exe`, perform the following steps:

1. Type `$PSVersionTable`.

2. Press *Enter*.

3. You will see that the PowerShell (PS) Version is **PSVersion 3.0**:

Method 3 – the Host Version property

After starting `Powershell.exe`, perform the following steps:

1. Type `$Host.Version`.

2. Press *Enter*.

3. You will see that the Major version is **3**:

By this point, you should have PowerShell 3.0 installed and properly configured on your computer.

Quick start – PowerShell 3.0 WMI basics

One of the biggest changes you will see in the PowerShell 3.0 release is the new CIM cmdlets for remote management. In the previous versions of PowerShell, the WMI cmdlets were executed through a protocol known as **Distributed Component Object Model** (**DCOM**). It is a proprietary Microsoft protocol and bound to the WMI cmdlets that are able to work with the Windows operating systems. Since this did not provide for interoperability with the other CIM-based servers, Microsoft introduced **Web Services for Management** (**WS-Man**) cmdlets for use with non-Windows-based systems. The problem with the WS-Man cmdlets, however, is that they are SOAP-based, and don't provide a user-friendly experience within PowerShell.

Using the basic CIM cmdlets

The new CIM cmdlets blend the best of both worlds with DCOM and WS-Man. The CIM cmdlets utilize DCOM for local connections and the new WinRM (Microsoft's version of WS-Man) for remote connections. Since both DCOM and WinRM are tightly integrated into PowerShell, it provides for better remote management of Windows/non-Windows-based systems and makes WMI/CIM manipulation a breeze.

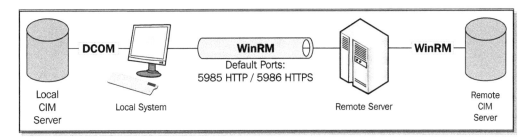

The first set of CIM cmdlets that you will learn about convert a session to a local or a remote system. While a session is not required for use with the other CIM cmdlets, it is recommended to use a session. A session helps broker communications with the remote systems, where the connection between them may be unreliable. A session can also avoid any commands being executed locally instead of remotely or vice versa.

Lastly, a session can be created to execute the same set of commands on multiple systems at the same time, instead of executing them individually.

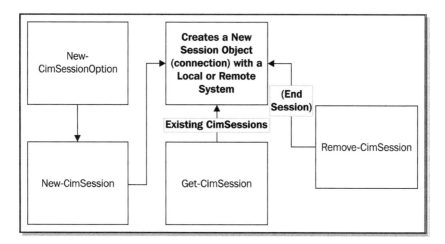

✦ **The New-CimSession (alias: ncms) cmdlet**: This creates a new session object (connection) with a single or multiple CIM servers. This session is used to broker communications between the source and destination systems. The New-CimSession cmdlet has a variety of cmdlet triggers, which aid in establishing the connection between systems. These include selecting authentication protocols, passing credentials, specifying session timeouts and connection port numbers, and creating a user-friendly name to reference the session or a group of sessions.

✦ **The New-CimSessionOption (alias: ncso) cmdlet**: This is used in conjunction with the New-CimSession cmdlet to create a new session option object. The New-CimSessionOption cmdlet allows you to specify items such as session protocol (DCOM/WSMAN), proxy information, user interface language, packet integrity, packet encoding, packet privacy, and other related connection-specific items. This provides for a more granular connection string to the CIM servers. This is not, however, required to make a connection.

✦ **The Get-CimSession (alias: gcms) cmdlet**: This retrieves the current session objects (connections) associated with the PowerShell instance (the current PowerShell window executing code). This allows you to retrieve the existing session objects that are created between the source and destination systems and execute code against the session.

✦ **The Remove-CimSession (alias: rcms) cmdlet**: This terminates or ends the current session object. The Remove-CimSession cmdlet is versatile as it can terminate an ID, Name, ComputerName, or InstanceID parameter.

Creating, verifying, and terminating new sessions

In this section, you will learn how to create a new session to the local computer. You will then create another new session to the local computer forcing the WSMAN protocol. You will then create multiple sessions using the -Name trigger, emulating multiple system connections and grouping the connections. After creating the sessions, you will query the existing sessions, and terminate the sessions by ID and Name.

To create a local session:

1. Open a new PowerShell window.

2. To create a new CIM session, type the following command and press *Enter*:

   New-CimSession

3. After creating a new session, you will see that the new **Id**, **Name**, and **InstanceID** unique identifiers are created, with the computer name of **localhost** using the **DCOM** protocol:

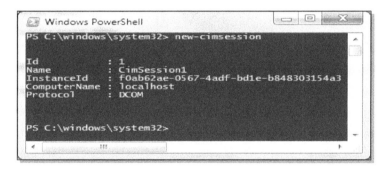

Now let's create a session with the New-CimSessionOption cmdlet. By manually setting the new-cimsession option of -Protocol, you can force the local CIM connection to use WSMAN instead of DCOM. When issuing the $SessionOption= variable ahead of the command, it stores the new session object in that variable for use with the New-CimSession cmdlet and the -SessionOption trigger.

To create a local session using the WSMAN protocol:

1. Create the new CIM session option object by typing the following command and press *Enter*:

   ```
   $SessionOption = New-CimSessionOption -Protocol WSMAN
   ```

2. To create the new CIM session with the new CIM session option, type the following command and press *Enter*:

   ```
   New-CimSession -SessionOption $SessionOption
   ```

3. After creating a new session, you will see that the new Id, Name, and InstanceID unique identifiers are created, with the ComputerName identifier of localhost using the WSMAN protocol.

There may be instances where you want to connect to multiple systems of the related functions at the same time. This would allow you to execute a script simultaneously on these systems. In the next part, you will make multiple connections in a single command, and label them WebServers.

 While you are making multiple connections to the localhost in this example, you can replace each localhost with different server names for use in your environment. The command will create individual connections to each of these systems, but will group them with the –NAME trigger of WebServers.

4. To create a new session to multiple systems, use a comma separator between the systems. To complete this action, type the following command and press *Enter*:

   ```
   New-CimSession -Computer localhost,localhost,localhost -Name
   WebServers
   ```

5. After creating multiple new sessions, you will see the creation of unique **Id** and **InstanceID** identifiers, with the computer names of **localhost** using the **WSMAN** protocol, and they are grouped as **WebServers**:

Once you create the new sessions, you can use the Get-CimSession cmdlet to retrieve these existing session objects. When you retrieve the existing sessions, you have the ability to execute code against these sessions. The Get-CimSession cmdlet allows you to retrieve these sessions by using their Id, Name, ComputerName, and InstanceID identifiers. This is helpful in instances where you want to execute different tasks on different sessions or while sequencing an upgrade. In this example, we will learn how to retrieve all of the sessions, learn how to retrieve sessions by ID, by computer name, and by grouped name.

1. To retrieve all of the sessions, type the following command and press *Enter*:

   ```
   Get-CimSession
   ```

2. To retrieve all of the sessions matching the ID number of 1, type the following command and press *Enter*:

   ```
   Get-CimSession -ID 1
   ```

3. To retrieve all of the sessions matching the computer name of localhost, type the following command and press *Enter*:

   ```
   Get-CimSession -ComputerName localhost
   ```

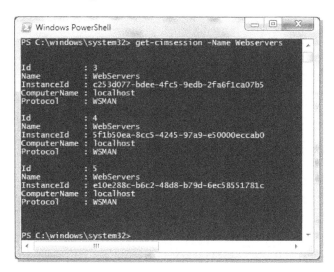

4. To retrieve all of the sessions matching the -Name value of WebServers, type the following command and press *Enter*:

   ```
   Get- CimSession -Name WebServers
   ```

It is best practice to remove the session objects after you are done utilizing them. This ensures that the scripts don't execute on the wrong sessions and also prevents session exploits. In this example, you will remove the sessions by ID number, by name, by computer name, and verify that there are no sessions after executing Get-CIMSession.

1. To remove the session matching the ID of 1, type the following command and press *Enter*:

   ```
   Remove-CimSession -ID 1
   ```

2. To remove the session matching the name of WebServers, type the following command and press *Enter*:

   ```
   Remove-CimSession -Name WebServers
   ```

3. To remove the session matching the computer name of localhost, type the following command and press *Enter*:

   ```
   Remove-CimSession -ComputerName LocalHost
   ```

4. To verify that there are no open sessions, type the following command and press *Enter*:

   ```
   Get-CimSession
   ```

5. The session objects are removed when the command doesn't provide any results:

Top features you'll want to know about

PowerShell is an object-oriented development language. When using PowerShell, you have the ability to call classes that read, store, and manipulate items on a system. A class is like a set of instructions and it's comprised of members. Two of the most commonly used members in a class are **properties** (read and store) and **methods** (execute). The call of a class isn't a direct reference to that object. Calling a class creates a copy of that object, called an **instance**. The instance is then referenced to interact with the class members. PowerShell 3.0 introduces new CIM instance cmdlets that enable you to work with classes, members, and instances. As you work through the new PowerShell cmdlets, it's important to remember that you are referencing instances of class objects and storing them into variables. This is very different from the command-line where the actual text values are being stored in a declared variable.

 It is recommended to utilize the CIM cmdlets with a session to broker communications with the CIM servers. As you create scripts for your environment, remember to create CIM sessions before executing commands.

New CIM instance and class cmdlets

The WMI structure is a hierarchical layout that has connecting class references or associations between classes. Sorting through the classes can be cumbersome due to the number of classes available. The Get-CimClass (alias: gcls) cmdlet has been created to provide robust searching capabilities within the WMI structure. The Get-CimClass cmdlet allows you to retrieve different classes by sorting through the different attributes of these classes.

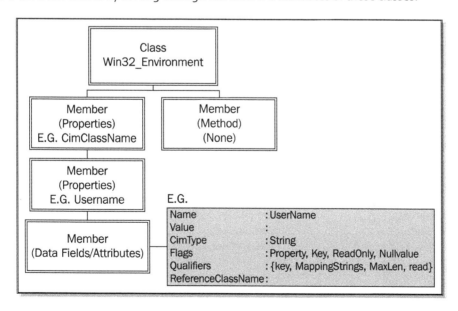

Classes have a variety of members that you can interact with to obtain information from the CIM server. The preceding diagram displays a sample hierarchy of the Win32_Environment class. As you can see in the diagram, the Win32_Environment class has properties; those properties in turn have properties. When you get further into the hierarchy, you will get to the data fields or attributes of that property.

> You will use this hierarchy as a reference when you are working through the Get-CimClass cmdlet examples.

When you first enter the Get-CimClass command in PowerShell, you will receive a listing of over 1000 class names. To trim this record set, you can use a technique known as piping. The pipe (|) character tells PowerShell to take the existing set of information and groom it to a more specific record set.

For example, execute the following command:

```
Get-CimClass | where {$_.CimClassName -match "Environment"}
```

Here, you execute the Get-CimClass cmdlet and groom it to only select the CimClassName values that contain the word Environment. You will see that the lists of thousands are now reduced to just two results:

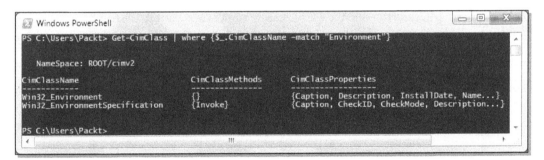

When you determine what class you would like to work with, for example Win32_Environment, you have the ability to view additional information about the properties and members of that class. To perform this, you use the Get-CimClass cmdlet to query the Win32_Environment class:

```
Get-CimClass Win32_Environment
```

You will see that the Win32_Environment class has the properties of CimClassName, CimMethodName, and CimClassProperties. You will also see that the CimClassProperties class property has some properties of its own (Caption, Description, InstallDate and so on):

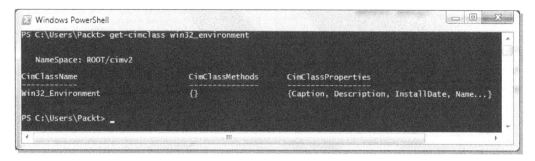

This query is different from the first query as, in the first query, you are obtaining the classes that have the word `Environment`. The second query evaluates the `Win32_Environment` class for its members and their properties.

Execute the following command to retrieve the list of `CimClassProperties`:

Get-CimClass Win32_Environment | foreach-object CimClassProperties

When you do so, you can see the different attributes for `CimClassProperties`, which include `Name`, `Value`, `CimType`, `Flags`, `Qualifiers`, and `ReferenceClassName`. Some of these attributes contain values, while others are null and contain no data.

```
Windows PowerShell
PS C:\Users\Packt> Get-CimClass Win32_Environment | foreach-object cimclassproperties

Name               : Caption
Value              :
CimType            : String
Flags              : Property, ReadOnly, NullValue
Qualifiers         : {MaxLen, read}
ReferenceClassName :

Name               : Description
Value              :
CimType            : String
Flags              : Property, ReadOnly, NullValue
Qualifiers         : {read}
ReferenceClassName :

Name               : InstallDate
Value              :
CimType            : DateTime
Flags              : Property, ReadOnly, NullValue
Qualifiers         : {MappingStrings, read}
ReferenceClassName :
```

All of these attributes define how a computer system can interact with the WMI. For example, `Caption` has a `ReadOnly` flag attribute. This means that the `Caption` attribute is an attribute that cannot be changed.

Get-CimClass cmdlets

The Get-CimInstance (alias: gcim) cmdlet is designed to retrieve WMI information from an instance of a class. The Get-CimInstance cmdlet has the ability to retrieve and execute the same class members as the Get-WMIObject cmdlets; however, it leverages the ability to query and execute over sessions. It also provides access to query non-Windows-based systems for CIM information.

The Get-CimInstance cmdlet is designed to retrieve information from the WMI. An example is querying the Win32_computersystem class using Get-CimInstance. By using the cmdlet, you can derive the computer name, primary owner name, domain name, and other information stored in the WMI pertaining to the system.

The following example creates a session with the local computer, and then queries the win32_computersystem class through that session for its members and properties. After the query, the CIM session is terminated and removed.

```
$session = new-CimSession

Get-CimInstance Win32_computersystem –CimSession $session

Remove-CimSession $session
```

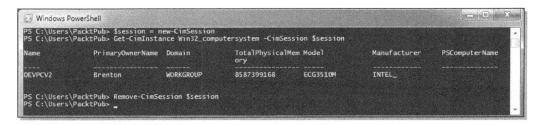

New-CimInstance cmdlets

The New-CimInstance (alias: ncim) cmdlet allows you to add new data field variables to classes. These data field variables will remain persistent and will be accessible by anyone who connects to the CIM server. This is helpful in instances where you'll need to store a setting on the system, but don't want to store it in the registry or the filesystem.

Not all classes allow you to create new instances or data field variables in them. The Win32_Environment property is one that enables you to add data field variables to the class.

For example, consider the following command:

```
New-CimInstance Win32_Environment -Property @{Name="ComputerWarranty";Var
iableValue="Expires 5 June 2018"; UserName="Packt\PacktUser"}
```

```
Get-Ciminstance win32_environment | Where {$_.name -match
"ComputerWarranty"}
```

This creates a new CIM instance data field variable within Win32_Environment. The data field variable is named ComputerWarranty and places the value of Expires 5 June 2018 in the data field variable. The last attribute required is the UserName attribute, which needs to be a valid username. When you run the Get-CimInstance cmdlet, it will validate the variables to ensure that they are of proper syntax and have valid data types.

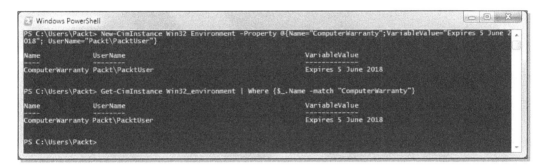

 Upon submission of the new CIM instance, the system will validate the fields. If there is an invalid username or you create an erroneous field, you will receive a **Generic Failure** error.

Set-CimInstance cmdlet

There may be instances where you create a data field and need to modify the contents of the data field. The Set-CimInstance (alias: scim) cmdlet is utilized to change the data fields of instances. This cmdlet can only be used on properties and instances that have a write qualifier attribute or are mapped to an additional qualifier.

To validate if a data field variable or instance have a `write` qualifier attribute, you can perform the following:

```
Get-cimclass Win32_environment | foreach-object cimclassproperties |
where {$_.Name -match "Name" -OR $_.Name -eq "VariableValue"}
```

When searching inside `Win32_Environment`, you will see that some of the properties have the `write` attribute while others don't. For those that do not have the `write` attribute, you will not be able to change them using the `Set-CimInstance` cmdlet. To change these attributes, you can create a new instance of that class, and set that value appropriately. Since we know that we can modify the `VariableValue` attribute for every `write` qualifier, we will continue to the next step.

Part 1 – pre-staging for Set-CimInstance

Part 1 creates a new data field with the name `ComputerWarranty` and the value of `Expires 5 June 2018`. This will be used for modification in part 2. If you've already created the data field, you may receive an error message about the object already existing.

Type the following code in PowerShell to prestage the environment:

```
New-CimInstance Win32_Environment -Property @{Name="ComputerWarranty";Var
iableValue="Expires 5 June 2018"; UserName="Packt\PacktUser"}
```

Part 2 – using the Set-CimInstance cmdlet

To start modifying an existing instance, you will utilize the `Get-CimInstance` cmdlet to call the `ComputerWarranty` data field and set it to the `$instance` variable. You then utilize the `Set-CimInstance` cmdlet to change the `ComputerWarranty` data field to `Expires 15 June 2020`. To verify that your changes were successful, you then run the `Get-CimInstance` command again:

```
$instance = Get-CimInstance Win32_Environment | where {$_.name -match
"ComputerWarranty"}

Set-CimInstance $instance -Property @{VariableValue="Expires 15 June
2020"}

Get-CimInstance Win32_Environment | Where {$_.name -match
"ComputerWarranty"}
```

Here is the output:

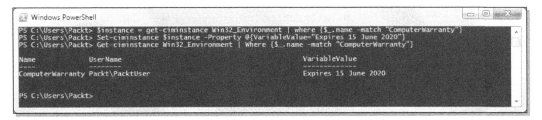

Remove-CimInstance cmdlets

It is best practice to remove the created instances and data fields that are no longer needed. The `Remove-CimInstance` (alias: `rcim`) cmdlets are used for removing these CIM instances and data fields.

Execute the following command:

```
$instance = Get-CimInstance Win32_Environment | Where {$_.name -match
"ComputerWarranty"}

$instance

PAUSE

Remove-CimInstance -ciminstance $instance

Get-Ciminstance win32_environment | Where {$_.name -match
"ComputerWarranty"}
```

Take a look at the following screenshot to understand the flow of executing the preceding commands:

To start the removal of an object, you will need to call the object that you want to remove. Utilize the Get-CimInstance cmdlet to call the ComputerWarranty data field and store the object into a variable named $instance. Since it is important that you verify the data that you are removing, you should display the instance contents by using $instance and PAUSE to halt the PowerShell execution. If the information is correct, press *Enter* on the keyboard. If the information is incorrect, you can exit by pressing *Ctrl + C* on the keyboard. The final step in the preceding script is the removal of the data field. You will use the Remove-CimInstance cmdlet and then use the Get-CimInstance cmdlet to verify that the data is actually gone from the CIM server.

Get-CimAssociatedInstance cmdlet

The Get-CimAssociatedInstance (alias: gcai) cmdlet provides the ability to better search through the WMI structure to find the CIM classes that are associated to each other. Once you find the classes that are associated, you have the ability to link those classes to specific instances and correlate the data. A good example to explain the association process is with Windows services. You will need to determine which Windows Service classes have associations. To do so, execute the following command:

```
$cimname = Get-CimClass -ClassName *Service* -Qualifier "Association"
$cimname.CimClassName
```

First, you will start by executing the Get-CimClass command with the ClassName variable of *service* and a qualifier of Association. This tells the Get-CimClass cmdlet to find any classes that have the text "service" in them, and those that have "associated" members or properties. You will then print the CimClassNames values to the screen to determine which class you want to work with. You will see that there are a lot of classes that are associated with service wildcard; however, the specific class instance you want to work with is Win32_DependentService.

```
Windows PowerShell                                              _ □ X
PS C:\Users\PacktPub> $c = Get-CimClass -ClassName *Service* -Qualifier "Association"
PS C:\Users\PacktPub> $c.CimClassName
Win32_ServiceSpecificationService
Win32_SystemServices
Win32_LoadOrderGroupServiceMembers
CIM_ServiceAccessBySAP
CIM_BootServiceAccessBySAP
CIM_ClusterServiceAccessBySAP
Win32_LoadOrderGroupServiceDependencies
CIM_HostedService
CIM_HostedBootService
CIM_DeviceServiceImplementation
CIM_ServiceServiceDependency
Win32_DependentService
CIM_SoftwareFeatureServiceImplementation
CIM_ServiceSAPDependency
PS C:\Users\PacktPub> _
```

Now execute the following:

```
$service = Get-CimInstance Win32_Service | where {$_.name -match
"Winmgmt"}
```

```
$service = Get-CimAssociatedInstance -InputObject $Service -Association
Win32_DependentService
```

```
$Service.Caption
```

The `Win32_DependentService` class will provide the association information of the
dependent services for any Windows service. By utilizing the `Get-CimAssociatedInstance`
cmdlet, we can make a correlation between the Windows Management (`wmgmt`) service and
the other dependency services on the system. In the last step of the code, you will display the
associated services caption property for easy determination of service names.

```
Administrator: Windows PowerShell                                          □ □ X
PS C:\Users\Packt> $service = Get-CimInstance Win32_Service | where {$_.name -match "Winmgmt"}
PS C:\Users\Packt> $service = Get-CimAssociatedInstance -InputObject $Service -Association Win32_DependentService
PS C:\Users\Packt> $Service.Caption
Remote Procedure Call (RPC)
SMS Agent Host
IP Helper
Internet Connection Sharing (ICS)
SMS Task Sequence Agent
Security Center
PS C:\Users\Packt>
```

Invoke-CimMethod cmdlet

The `Invoke-CimMethod` (alias: `icim`) cmdlet allows you to invoke a method associated with
a class. When you invoke a method, you start an action associated with that CIM class. After
completion, the method will provide a return value, which will indicate the success or failure
of the method execution.

For example:

```
Invoke-CimMethod Win32_Process -MethodName "Create" -Arguments @{
CommandLine = 'calc.exe'}
Invoke-CimMethod -Query 'select * from Win32_Process where name like
"calc.exe"' -MethodName "Terminate"
```

The `Invoke-CimMethod` cmdlet is responsible for triggering actions on the system. In the previous example, we used the `Invoke-CimMethod` cmdlet to invoke the `Create` method, which will create a new calculator instance. In the second command, we used the `Invoke-CimMethod` cmdlet to invoke the `Terminate` method, which will terminate all instance names that match with `calc.exe`.

Scenario 1 – using WMI in software deployment

When you are deploying software, there are many things to consider. For example, when you deploy software to a set of systems that have different operating systems or hardware platforms, you may require different prerequisite software. This can cause issues during the deployment process, and ultimately create a supportability nightmare.

This section goes over the different tasks that may need to be performed during software deployment. While this section is not all inclusive, it will provide a quick reference to the materials you may need as you are developing your deployment scripts.

Checking the operating system version

All software packages have different operating system requirements. Some installers look for specific operating systems, and if they are not present, the installation will fail. Others will bundle x86 and x64 drivers in separate installers and it may result in the installation of the wrong operating system architecture. This section explains the process by which you can derive the operating system version and operating system architecture of your system.

Not all WMI queries within PowerShell 3.0 are as clear-cut as pulling a single value. Obtaining the operating system type is definitely one of these queries. A popular method for obtaining the operating system type is by retrieving the `BuildNumber` and `Caption` values from the `Win32_OperatingSystem` class:

```
$os = get-ciminstance win32_operatingsystem
If ($os.BuildNumber -eq "7601" -and $os.Caption -match "7") { Write-Host
"This system is Windows 7 x64" }
```

The preceding example provides a method by which one can determine the operating system based on the `BuildNumber` and `Caption` values from the `Win32_OperatingSystem` class. You could just retrieve the caption, but often it wouldn't identify system architecture, so the PowerShell community uses this technique instead.

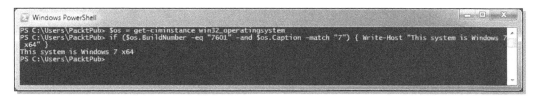

A variety of combinations exist to identify the operating system types, some of which are as follows:

Operating system	BuildNumber value	Caption value
Windows XP 32-bit	2600	
Windows XP 64-bit	3790	XP
Windows Server 2003	3790	2003
Windows Vista 32	6000	
Windows Vista 64-bit	6001	Vista
Windows Server 2008 32-bit	6001	2008
Windows 7 32-bit	7600	
Windows 7 64-bit	7601	7
Windows Server 2008 R2	7601	2008

For Windows 8 and Windows Server 2012, the method of obtaining the operating system type and architecture is slightly different. This is due to Microsoft resyncing the build numbers across the operating systems.

For Windows 8

You will see that for Windows 8, you need to retrieve the `BuildNumber` and `OSArchitecture` properties to determine the operating system type. The following code example gets the `win32_operatingsystem` class and places the object into the `$os` variable. It then queries the `BuildNumber` and `OSArchitecture` properties to verify the operating system. This call can be changed to check for a 32-bit operating system by using `$os.OSArchitecture -match "32-bit"`.

```
$os = get-ciminstance win32_operatingsystem

If ($os.BuildNumber -eq "9200" -and $os.OSArchitecture -match "64-bit") {
Write-Host "This system is Windows 8 x64" }
```

Windows Server 2012

For Windows Server 2012, you will only need to use the `BuildNumber` and `Caption` properties, like in the prior operating systems. The following is the reference information for Windows 8 and Windows Server 2012 operating systems:

Operating systems	BuildNumber	OSArchitecture	Caption
Windows 8 32-bit	9200	`32 bit`	
Windows 8 64-bit	9200	`64 bit`	
Windows Server 2012 64-bit	9200		2012

Here is an example for Windows Server 2012:

```
$os = get-ciminstance win32_operatingsystem

If ($os.BuildNumber -eq "9200" -and $os.Caption -match "2012") { Write-
Host "This system is Server 2012" }
```

And here is the output:

Checking disk space

It is common when deploying software to check that there is an appropriate amount of disk space. Between the software deployment or update, logfiles, and database growth, it's important to verify the disk requirements during a deployment. This section explains the best method to check for disk space.

Here is an example:

```
$diskobject = Get-ciminstance win32_logicaldisk | where {$_.DeviceID -eq
"C:"}

if ($diskobject.freespace -gt 1GB) { Write-Host "Disk is larger than 1 GB
- Execute Code!" }
```

The example shown here calls the `win32_logicaldisk` class, which reports all of the logical disks on the system. It then selects the object where the `DeviceID` attribute is equal to the drive letter of C. After that, it performs an `IF` statement query to check whether the `FreeSpace` attribute of the device with the drive letter C is greater than 1 GB. If it is, it will proceed to the subsequent lines of your code. In this case, it just writes text to the screen:

This call can be modified to evaluate free space in GB-, MB-, and KB-friendly denotations. This call is also dynamic in the sense that you can select items by `$_.DriveType`. The drive type number correlates to different storage types. The `DriveType` property specifies the following about the drive:

+ A `DriveType` property of 0 denotes an unknown drive type
+ A `DriveType` property of 1 denotes a removable drive
+ A `DriveType` property of 2 denotes a fixed drive
+ A `DriveType` property of 3 denotes a network drive
+ A `DriveType` property of 4 denotes a CD-ROM drive
+ A `DriveType` property of 5 denotes a RAM-Disk drive

Checking the hardware model number

During software deployment, there are instances where you need to know the model number of the workstation or server you are working on. This may be because you need to deploy a model-specific driver or shim to the system. This section explains the best method to obtain the model number of a system.

Execute the following:

```
$pc = get-ciminstance win32_computersystem
Write-host "Model Number of System is:" $pc.Model
```

This example leverages the `win32_computersystem` class to pull the computer model number from the CIM server. The model number is then printed to the screen using the `write-host` command:

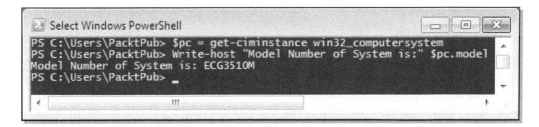

Checking for running processes

When deploying software, it's important to ensure that the existing software instances or software dependencies are not currently running. This will help avoid files and registry entries being locked due to the processes running in memory. This section will show how to determine if a process or multiple processes are running in memory.

Execute the following code:

```
Function Query-Process { param($pname)
$process = Get-CimInstance win32_process | where {$_.name -match
$pname}


IF ($process) {
If ($process.count -gt "1") { Write-host "Multiple instances of
$pname Are Running"
}
    Else { Write-Host "A single instance of $pname is running" }
}
Else { Write-Host "There are no running processes that match $pname"}
}

Query-Process "Powershell.exe"
Query-Process "ThisDoesNotExist.exe"
```

When you are creating scripts that will need to be executed multiple times, it is a common practice to create a function for executing the same code multiple times.

This example creates a new function named Query-Process. The param command takes the process name passed into the function and assigns it to the $pname variable. The next step in the process is to call the win32_process class and match any values that contain the text in $pname.

The first IF statement will evaluate if it returns any processes at all. If the result is null, the script will know that there are no processes that match the name running and will skip to the else statement. In the instance that there are processes running, the function will issue a second IF statement to determine how many processes are running on that system. If there is more than one process running, it will report that there are multiple instances. If there is only one instance, it will state that there is only one instance.

You can easily modify this code to terminate the processes instead of printing text on the screen. If you want to terminate the process, you can use either the Remove-CimInstance cmdlet that you learned earlier or you can use the taskkill.exe tool. With taskkill.exe, you may also choose to terminate by ProcessID if you don't want to terminate all instances of that process.

Here is the output of executing the preceding code:

```
PS C:\Users\Packt> Function Query-Process { param($pname)
>> $process = Get-CimInstance win32_process | where {$_.name -match
>> $pname}
>>
>> IF ($process) {
>> If ($process.count -gt "1") { Write-host "Multiple instances of
>> $pname Are Running"
>> }
>> Else { Write-Host "A single instance of $pname is running" }
>> }
>> Else { Write-Host "There are no running processes that match $pname"}
>> }
>>
PS C:\Users\Packt> Query-Process "Powershell.exe"
A single instance of Powershell.exe is running
PS C:\Users\Packt> Query-Process "ThisDoesNotExist.exe"
There are no running processes that match ThisDoesNotExist.exe
PS C:\Users\Packt>
```

Remember that when you are using these functions, you have to define them before using them. You only have to define them once per script, which makes them useful in situations where you need to repeat the function multiple times.

Checking for running services

Similar to checking for running processes, there are multiple scenarios where you would want to make sure whether a process is running or not, on the system for deployment. A good example is using a load balancer and performing a dynamic code push to multiple servers in that load balance pool. You have the ability to fail (or stop) the service on one server in the pool, and verify that the service starts successfully on another server in the pool prior to the code upgrade.

PowerShell introduced the `Get-Service`, `Set-Service`, `Stop-Service`, and `Start-Service` cmdlets, which allow you to get and manipulate services through cmdlets. This section of the code is an alternative method to obtain the state of a service and show the difference in the output from the commands. There are many instances where the built-in cmdlets don't provide all the information required to manage the system. For example, the `Get-Service` cmdlet only provides a partial listing of the information pertaining to the service. This is in comparison to the `Get-CimInstance` cmdlet, which provides a much more detailed look into the service.

> This is a result of the `Get-Service` cmdlet using the `System.ServicesProcess.ServiceController` assembly and the WMI query accessing the `Microsoft.Management.Infrastructure.CimInstance`. While both calls are accessing information pertaining to a service, one will return a more detailed look at the service. This provides value to those who need to interact with a service in a more detailed manner.

1. The first step is to define the service name in a variable:

   ```
   $sname = "W32Time"
   ```

2. The next step in the process is to use the `Get-Service` cmdlet to query for the W32Time service. This will be used only for comparison purposes between WMI and the built-in cmdlet.

   ```
   Get-Service $sname
   ```

3. You will then make a call to the `Win32_Service` class and match any values that contain the text in `$sname`:

   ```
   $service = get-ciminstance win32_service | where {$_.name -match $sname}

   $service
   ```

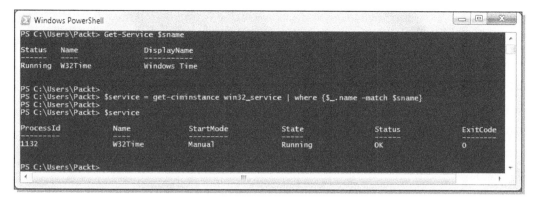

While it may be an easier syntax to use the service cmdlets, you may need to still leverage the CIM code to dig deeper into the running services and their dependencies.

Viewing the installed software

Most software packages leverage the Windows Installer Service to install themselves on a system. When using the Windows Installer Service, detailed information pertaining to the software is stored within the CIM server. This information can then be queried later and used to derive the existing software on the system.

When installing software to a variety of systems, it is not uncommon to find the software dependencies missing from those systems. Creating a query to check for dependencies is helpful in these instances to install these items.

The `Win32_Product` class contains the software that is installed on the system. This class has several properties that you can use to identify software packages. When working with software installers, it is best practice to use the `IdentifyingNumber` attribute. The `IdentifyingNumber` attribute is a unique GUID that is associated with a software package upon the creation of that software installer. The attribute will ensure that you have all of the required dependencies.

To do so, execute the following command:

```
$SilverlightGUID = "{89F4137D-6C26-4A84-BDB8-2E5A4BB71E00}"
$Silverlight = Get-CimInstance win32_product | where {$_.name -match
"Microsoft Silverlight"}
If ($silverlight.IdentifyingNumber -match $SilverlightGUID) {
Write-Host "The Silverlight Software is Installed. Dependency Check
Successful."
}
Else {
Write-Host "Error: Silverlight Not Installed. Dependency Check Failed."
}
```

Microsoft Silverlight is a common requirement among the Windows Presentation Foundation applications. This example provides the method by which we can check the installed GUID against the expected GUID of Microsoft Silverlight. We first set the expected Silverlight GUID variable to the expected GUID. We then query the `Win32_product` class and match any names that contain the words "Microsoft Silverlight". After that, we compare the expected value with the current value, and we print whether the dependency check was successful or a failure:

```
$Silverlight = Get-CimInstance win32_product | where {$_.name -match
"Microsoft Silverlight"}

Write-Host "The Installed GUID of Silverlight Is" $silverlight.
IdentifyingNumber
```

Here is the output:

Remember that when you try this section of code, the Silverlight GUID may be different on your computer or on the destination computers. The given code snippet provides a method to check the installed Silverlight version on your computer.

Checking file version numbers

Not all software packages make installation entries within the CIM server. This may be because they are a native component of the operating system, use an antiquated packaging utility, or don't leverage a packaging utility for installation. To work around this issue, you can check the file version numbers and compare them with the expected values. This section will provide an example of how to compare version numbers.

```
$IExplorer = Get-ciminstance -Query "Select * from CIM_Datafile where
name = 'c:\\Program Files\\Internet Explorer\\iexplore.exe'"
```

```
if ($IExplorer.Version -lt 8)   { Write-Host "Error! Minimum Internet
Explorer Version Dependency Check Failed with Version: " $IExplorer.
version
}
```

```
if ($IExplorer.Version -gt 8) {
Write-host "Minimum Internet Explorer Version Dependency Check Passed
with Version: " $IExplorer.version
}
```

Internet Explorer is built into the Windows operating system. As a result, it does not have an entry in **Add/Remove Programs** and is not registered in the CIM server as an installed software package. Yet, there are many applications that rely on the Internet Explorer version to be at a minimum version level. The preceding script utilizes the `Cim_DataFile` class to query the file information of the Internet Explorer executable. It then checks the system to see if it is at the minimum version level of 8. If it is not, it will provide an error message. If it is greater than version 8, it will succeed.

Scenario 2 – dynamically provisioning the systems

As data centers are moving more towards cloud-based technologies, the need to dynamically provision systems is growing. When you create systems that can dynamically provision themselves using a template, it greatly reduces the delivery time of servers and workstations to your environment. Not only will this provide for cost savings, but it also reduces your workload to just the configuration of the systems, without waiting for the build.

This scenario provides examples of the different activities you may need to perform during the creation of new operating system instances. This scenario provides methods to dynamically provision systems with minimum intervention from a system administrator.

When dynamically provisioning systems, it's important to set up different scripts to perform different items. This helps when you are trying to troubleshoot the build failures in your environment. It is recommended that you create separate scripts in this order:

+ `FirstStart.ps1`: Add this script to the unattended answer file prior to deployment of the operating system. This will be the first startup script of the system. It will install any dependencies, rename the computer, stage the second script, and restart the system.

+ `OSConfig.ps1`: This script will configure any items that are required by the operating system. These include items such as computer description, enabling of features, enabling firewall rules, and configuring network interfaces. The final step is to stage the third script. It may or may not be necessary to restart the system at this point depending on your activities.

* `AppConfig.ps1`: This script will configure any items that are required by the specific role of the system. This may include configuration of new features, execution of database scripts, creation of directories and registry entries, and the installation of the application on the system. This may also stage a cleanup script to complete the system. It may or may not be necessary to restart the system at this point depending on your activities.

* `CleanUp.ps1`: After the installation of new software and features, typically there are files and settings that need to be cleaned up. You can also set up any maintenance tasks during this phase for future supportability of the system.

Sequencing the scripts after a restart

The sequencing of scripts is necessary to ensure that different activities are completed in a very specific order. If you don't sequence scripts in the correct order, you may configure items of the operating system that change after subsequent scripts execute. This section provides a method for chaining scripts to withstand a reboot of the system. While this activity does not use a CIM cmdlet, it will provide you with the ability to chain your scripts that are using the CIM cmdlets.

```
# Run these Commands in a PowerShell Window Running as Administrator
$regpath = Get-Item "HKLM:\Software\Microsoft\Windows\CurrentVersion\
RunOnce"


Set-ItemProperty $regpath.PsPath OSBuildScript "c:\BuildScripts\OSConfig.
ps1"


$regpath
```

The best method to chain scripts to withstand a reboot of a system is through creating a registry entry in the `RunOnce` section of `HKEY_LOCAL MACHINE`. This is done by using the `Get-Item` and `Set-ItemProperties` cmdlets and by creating a new string to run the `C:\BuildScripts\OSConfig.ps1` PowerShell script on the next start of the system. If the configuration of this value doesn't work properly, you will receive an error message with the error reason.

Here is the output:

```
Administrator: Windows PowerShell
PS C:\Windows\system32> # Run these Commands in a PowerShell Window Running as Administrator
PS C:\Windows\system32> $regpath = Get-Item "HKLM:\Software\Microsoft\Windows\CurrentVersion\RunOnce"
PS C:\Windows\system32>
PS C:\Windows\system32> Set-ItemProperty $regpath.PsPath OSBuildScript "c:\BuildScripts\OSConfig.ps1"
PS C:\Windows\system32>
PS C:\Windows\system32> $regpath


    Hive: HKEY_LOCAL_MACHINE\Software\Microsoft\Windows\CurrentVersion


Name                           Property
----                           --------
RunOnce                        OSBuildScript : c:\BuildScripts\OSConfig.ps1


PS C:\Windows\system32>
```

Renaming the computer with a random name and a prefix

When you are creating a new operating system instance, you may want to name the computer with a prefix and random numbers. This section provides instructions on how to create seven random numbers after a prefix, and rename a computer to the new name utilizing a WMI method.

1. The first step in the process is to call a new `System.Random` object. This will be used to generate new random numbers:

   ```
   $random = New-object System.Random
   ```

2. The second step in the process is to create a loop. The `1..7` notation with a `ForEach` command is "shorthand" for saying repeat this step seven times.

   ```
   1..7 | ForEach {$RandNum = $RandNum + [char]$Random.Next(48,57) }
   ```

   We then populate the `$RandNum` with seven random numbers between the numbers zero (character `48`) and nine (character `57`).

3. In the next step we add the prefix of `Packt` to the random numbers and assign it to a new variable named `$newSystemName`.

   ```
   $newSystemName = "Packt" + $RandNum
   ```

4. To rename the system, you will use the `Get-WMIobject` cmdlet to call the `Win32_ComputerSystem` class and store it in the `$system` variable:

   ```
   $system = Get-wmiobject win32_ComputerSystem
   ```

5. We will execute the `Rename` method on the system and the computer will be renamed.

   ```
   $system.Rename($newSystemName)

   Write-Host "Your computer has been renamed to $newsystemname"
   ```

Waiting for service states

When you are building systems dynamically, you will run into instances where your next line of execution is dependent upon a running service. This section displays the proper method to query and wait for a service to start. You will also be able to specify a timeout period, so that your code doesn't hang indefinitely.

```
function QueryService { param($Service,$ServiceName,$State,$timer1)


  $success = ""
  for ($b=1; $b -lt $timer1; $b++) {


    $servicestat = get-service $Service
        $status = $servicestat.status
    percent = $b * (100 / $timer1)


Write-Progress -Activity "Waiting on $Service Service..."
-PercentComplete $percent -CurrentOperation "$b2 Seconds Remaining"
-Status "Current $servicename Status: $status"


      if ($status -eq $State) {
Write-Host "$Service Service Started Successfully: $status in $b Seconds"
[int]$b = $timer1
$success = "yes"
```

```
Write-Progress -Activity "Completed" -Status "Current $Service Status:
$status in $b Seconds" -Completed

      }

    start-sleep 1

 }


  if ($success -ne "yes") {
Write-Host "ERROR in Script: $Service Service Did Not Start In $timer1
Seconds. Current Status: $status"

  }
}


QueryService "Winmgmt" "Windows Management Instrumentation" "Running" 120
```

As you start working with dynamic provisioning of systems, you will quickly realize that the timing of execution is extremely important. This example provides a realistic scenario that you will encounter with Windows Management Instrumentation. When the computer first starts, the Windows Management Instrumentation service isn't immediately available due to its dependency services starting. While some systems start their services faster than others, if the WMI service is not running, you will not be able to execute any WMI queries and your scripts will fail.

The script provided in this example is created inside a function. This allows you to repeat the query of services multiple times during the execution of your script. The first step is to define the function and accept multiple parameters in the function. These parameters include $Service (service name), $ServiceName (service display name), $status (stopped, running), $timer1 (the seconds until timeout), and $Success (to define the variable).

After we define these properties, we create the countdown loop. The loop syntax starts when $b equals 1. As long as $b is less than $timer1 (the timer), proceed with the loop. Every time the function loops, it adds 1 to $b ($b++ in shorthand). We stop the loop when $b is greater than or equal to $timer1.

The next step is to get the current service status for use in the Write-Progress cmdlet. We will then calculate what percentage the operation has completed. This is done by taking the $timer1 variable's value and dividing it by 100. This percent is used for the progress meter in the Write-Progress cmdlet. The Write-Progress cmdlet will display on the screen until $status equals the current $state value of the service. When it does, it will proceed to the next line of code.

If the loop completes without $status becoming equal to $state of the service, it will report that the service did not start in the time allotted. You may also want to add a BREAK command after the error message to stop the execution of further code.

The use of the function also allows for you to wait until a service stops. Services such as **Internet Information Services** (**IIS**) often take a while to stop, and this script provides the ability to wait until the service completely stops before proceeding.

The following screenshot displays the output of executing the preceding command-line script:

Setting the computer description

There will be instances where you will want to set the description of the computer. Some organizations use this for warranty information, while others use it for geographical placement of the system. This section will guide you through the manipulation of the computer description.

```
Get-CimClass Win32_Environment | foreach-object cimclassproperties |
where {$_.name -match "description"}
```

To start with, we need to determine if the `Description` property is writable. To do this, we will query the `Win32_Environment` class utilizing the `Get-CimClass` cmdlet. We will then pipe the class results to view the individual properties and their attributes. From there, we pipe the results again only to select the property name of `Description`.

You can see from the results (displayed in the next screenshot) that the qualifiers for the `Description` property have the `write` attribute assigned to it. This means that you can modify the `Value` attribute of the `Description` property, and ultimately modify the `Description` field of the computer.

Now run these commands in a PowerShell Window running as an Administrator:

```
$instance = Get-CimInstance win32_OperatingSystem

Set-CimInstance $instance -Property @{Description="Your Server
Description" }

$instance.Description
```

To configure the description of the computer, we will create a new instance of the Win32_OperatingSystem class and store the created object in the $instance variable. From there, we use the Set-CimInstance cmdlet to set the Description property to Your Server Description. To validate that the Description field was set correctly, we call the Description property of the Win32_OperatingSystem class using the $instance.description command.

The following screenshot displays the output of the code:

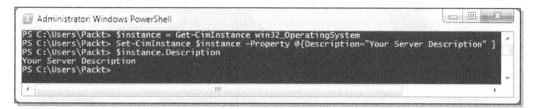

Scenario 3 – system maintenance

One of the most overlooked aspects of systems engineering is the execution of the maintenance tasks. This is often the result of new projects taking precedence over maintaining the existing systems. To reduce the risk in your environment, there are tasks that you may be able to automate, which will provide a hands-off approach to systems management.

Looking up the BIOS information

In most environments, the BIOS version is not consistent across the entire environment. This is a result of hardware manufacturers and distributers stocking inventory with the old BIOS versions and selling these systems to consumers. This section provides a quick snippet that allows you to determine the BIOS version and status.

The following code snippet provides the ability to view the current BIOS information. Here, we query the win32_bios class to obtain its properties. We then look at the Manufacturer, SMBiosVersion, SerialNumber, and Status properties. This is a simple script but very useful when attempting to maintain a uniform environment.

```
$bios = Get-ciminstance win32_bios


Write-Host "The Bios Manufacturer is:" $bios.Manufacturer
```

```
Write-Host "The Current Bios Version is:" $bios.SMBIOSBIOSVERSION
Write-Host "The Current Bios Serial Number is:" $bios.SerialNumber
Write-Host "The Current Bios Status is:" $bios.Status
```

Here is the output:

Looking at disk fragmentation

Disk fragmentation in corporations is highly common for a multitude of reasons. Through the use of PowerShell, you have the ability to script the defragmentation without a scheduled task. This creates the execute-on-demand process that provides information back to a system administrator about the fragmentation and end result of the defragmentation. This section explains the process by which you can remotely defragment a computer.

```
# Run This Command In A PowerShell Window Running As Administrator
$session = New-CimSession


$drive = get-ciminstance –cimsession $session –class win32_volume | where
{$_.DriveLetter -eq "c:"}


$report = Invoke-CimMethod –cimsession $session –InputObject $drive –name
DefragAnalysis

#Before You Get Object Properties, You Store the Recommendation in A var
$defrag = $report.DefragRecommended


$report = $report.DefragAnalysis


Write-Host "The File Fragmentation is" $Report.FilePercentFragmentation
"for a Total Fragmentation of" $Report.TotalPercentFragmentation "%"


if ($defrag -eq "True") { defrag c: /F }
```

The first section of this example sets up a new CIM session. This will be used to broker communications with the local disk drives of the system in which you want to determine fragmentation. You will then need to obtain the drive by which you want to query for fragmentation. In your example, you will be looking at C:. To invoke the CIM method for a fragmentation report, we invoke the `DefragAnalysis` method.

After the `DefragAnalysis` method completes its execution, it will come up with a defrag recommendation. This recommendation is the `DefragRecommended` property returned from the Defrag Analysis process. You also have the ability to return other properties native to the `DefragAnalysis` method, such as `FilePercentFragmentation` and `TotalPercentFragmentation`. If your `DefragRecommended` property is set to `True`, the script will defrag the C:.

```
Administrator: Windows PowerShell
PS C:\Users\Packt> # Run This Command In A PowerShell Window Running As Administrator
PS C:\Users\Packt> $session = New-CimSession
PS C:\Users\Packt>
PS C:\Users\Packt>
PS C:\Users\Packt> $drive = get-ciminstance -cimsession $session -class win32_volume | where {$_.DriveLetter -eq "c:"}
PS C:\Users\Packt>
PS C:\Users\Packt>
PS C:\Users\Packt> $report = Invoke-CimMethod -cimsession $session -InputObject $drive -name DefragAnalysis
PS C:\Users\Packt>
PS C:\Users\Packt> #Before You Get Object Properties, You Store the Recommendation in A var
PS C:\Users\Packt> $defrag = $report.DefragRecommended
PS C:\Users\Packt>
PS C:\Users\Packt> $report = $report.DefragAnalysis
PS C:\Users\Packt>
PS C:\Users\Packt> Write-Host "The File Fragmentation is" $Report.FilePercentFragmentation "for a Total Fragmentation of
" $Report.TotalPercentFragmentation "%"
The File Fragmentation is 0 for a Total Fragmentation of 0 %
PS C:\Users\Packt>
PS C:\Users\Packt> if ($defrag -eq "True") { defrag c: /F }
PS C:\Users\Packt>
```

System uptime

There are multiple instances where systems unexpectedly stop functioning. Many a time, the systems automatically restart. Until you sign into the system again, you won't know that it went down. In the instances where you don't have an operations management system, you may need a source for indications of problems with a system. This section provides a method to determine the system uptime, which may lead to the determination of the system's overall health.

```
$LastBootTime = (Get-CimInstance win32_OperatingSystem).LastBootUpTime
```

```
$uptime = (Get-Date) - $LastBootTime
```

```
Write-Host "System Has Been Running For" $uptime.days "Days," $uptime.
hours "Hours," $uptime.minutes "Minutes, and" $uptime.seconds "Seconds."
```

The best way to gather the system uptime involves a small amount of math. Since there is no direct value within WMI, you need to subtract two values to determine the uptime. Gather the `LastBootTime` property from the `Win32_operatingsystem` class. You will then get the current date and time, subtract the last boot time from it, and set it to the `$Uptime` variable.

Since the $Uptime variable has a type of datetime, you have the ability to directly convert the uptime values to **Days, Hours, Minutes**, and **Seconds** by just calling them as properties to the $Uptime variable, as shown in the next screenshot:

Reading error logs

Following the indications of system distress from system uptime, you have the ability, through WMI, to query the errors from the application and system logs. This is helpful when you want to determine if there are issues on a system which caused the system restart. This section provides instructions on how to look at the event log utilizing WMI and determine the number of errors over a period of seven days.

Please note that before starting this query and depending on the number of events that occurred, it may take a bit of time to generate the data. This is because of directly searching the event log on the system, which may take some time to generate.

1. The first step in this process is to get the current date and save it in the $date variable:

   ```
   $date = get-date
   ```

2. You will need to take the current date and subtract seven days from it to obtain seven days' worth of data. The datetime type doesn't have a subtract method, so you will add a negative number:

   ```
   $date = $date.AddDays(-7)
   ```

3. After that, you will query the Win32_NTLogEvent class and retrieve all Warning events that have the TimeGenerated attributes that are older than seven days. Since there will probably be a large result set, you don't need to print the entire record set to screen:

   ```
   $errors = get-ciminstance win32_ntlogevent | where {$_.Type -eq
   "Warning" -and $_.TimeGenerated -gt $date }
   ```

4. You will only print the count of warnings from the Event Log. In our example, there were 1159 warnings in the last seven days.

   ```
   If ($errors) { Write-Host "There Are Currently" $errors.count
   "Warnings in the Event Log" }
   ```

```
Administrator: Windows PowerShell
PS C:\Users\Packt> $date = get-date
PS C:\Users\Packt>
PS C:\Users\Packt> $date = $date.AddDays(-7)
PS C:\Users\Packt>
PS C:\Users\Packt> $errors = get-ciminstance win32_ntlogevent | where [$_.Type -eq "Warning" -and $_.TimeGenerated -gt $
date }
PS C:\Users\Packt>
PS C:\Users\Packt> If ($errors) { Write-Host "There Are Currently" $errors.count "Warnings in the Event Log" }
There Are Currently 1159 Warnings in the Event Log
PS C:\Users\Packt> _
```

Putting it all together

PowerShell is a dynamic scripting language and can be used in its many facets. Engineers, like yourself, are shifting their focus from manually maintaining systems to utilizing PowerShell for dynamic provisioning, management, and planned obsolescence of systems.

Provisioning of systems utilizing PowerShell 3.0 has become easier with the integration of the new CIM cmdlets. You may choose to query the CIM of a storage array host for the available space or you may want to determine the load of a virtualization host prior to provisioning. During the provisioning phase, you may choose to query the WMI for the model number of a system to apply specific updates or system drivers. After the provisioning phase, you may choose to run a system health check script to query the WMI for all of the Microsoft IIS application pools, ensuring they are in a running state.

Management of systems also has become easier with Windows Remote Management (WinRM) within the CIM cmdlets. You may choose to set up a management script that utilizes WMI to remotely query the Event Log of systems for the critical messages or failed login attempts. You may also want to locally query the WMI on systems for disk space, memory, or processor utilization and send an SNMP trap to a management system.

Planning for obsolescence with WMI is also a possibility by utilizing the WinRm and CIM cmdlets. You may also choose to create a PowerShell script to remotely pull, make, and model information of all the systems that are being planned for obsolescence. You may also choose to dynamically deprovision systems and check, utilizing WMI queries, that there are no active users on the systems.

You saw a multitude of methods by which you can utilize the new CIM cmdlets to manage systems. Since Windows Management Instrumentation is extremely dynamic, you have the ability to obtain limitless information pertaining to the systems you are working with.

This book has made you proficient in being able to install PowerShell 3.0 and Windows Management Framework on a system. You are now also able to create sessions using DCOM and Windows Remote Management. You can also remove sessions for avoiding accidental code execution.

The tools you gain in this book are a great foundation for the creation of your own PowerShell scripts. While the syntax of some of these commands may be difficult to pick up, you will find that, through practice, they can be picked up in a short period of time.

The biggest tip I can provide for PowerShell scripting is to start small and grow your scripts. A lot of the error messages within PowerShell don't provide detailed information. This creates a need for patience and small code snippets for troubleshooting. When your code is not working properly, search for an alternative method to do the same operation. Since PowerShell is so dynamic, you may be overcomplicating your calls that can be completed in fewer steps. Lastly, use the resources in the next section for researching scripts. The PowerShell community is growing every day and it's equally important to use it and to contribute to it.

Happy coding!

Do you need more information about the PowerShell CIM cmdlets? Try using the `get-help` cmdlet. For example, `Get-Help Get-CimSession`.

Do you need examples of how to use the cmdlets? Try updating the PowerShell help system by typing `update-help`.

People and places you should get to know

If you need help with PowerShell 3.0 – WMI, here are some people and places which will prove invaluable.

Official sites

✦ TechNet PowerShell homepage: `http://technet.microsoft.com/en-us/library/hh857339.aspx`

✦ Windows PowerShell blog: `http://blogs.msdn.com/b/powershell/`

✦ TechNet Scripting Library: `http://technet.microsoft.com/en-us/library/bb902776.aspx`

✦ Technet Learn Scripting: `http://technet.microsoft.com/en-us/dd793612`

Articles and tutorials

✦ This article was created by Brenton Blawat to explain encryption and decryption of user strings for usernames and passwords. This is helpful for use in scripts that need encrypted usernames and passwords for creating new CIM sessions:

`http://gallery.technet.microsoft.com/PowerShell-Script-410ef9df`

✦ For a detailed listing of the CIM classes, browse to `http://msdn.microsoft.com/library/windows/desktop/aa386179(v=vs.85).aspx`

Community

✦ Official forums: `http://social.technet.microsoft.com/Forums/en/category/scripting`

✦ Unofficial forums and PowerShell code repository: You can find the PowerShell Code Repository at `http://poshcode.org/`

✦ Open source project providing a framework for delivery of code using Microsoft Team Foundation Server and PowerShell: `https://github.com/eavonius/powerdelivery`

Blogs

✦ Brenton Blawat contributes to **Business and Information Technology (BIT)** Tangents blog, `http://www.bittangents.com`, which has PowerShell scripts for reference.

✦ Microsoft has several contributors to a section of their website called Hey, Scripting Guy! at `http://blogs.technet.com/b/heyscriptingguy/`. This website is full of useful snippets of code.

✦ Marc Van Orsouw, a Microsoft MVP for Windows Administration Framework, has a very popular blog located at `http://thepowershellguy.com/`. This is an excellent site for medium to advanced PowerShell scripters.

Twitter

✦ Follow Brenton Blawat, the author, at `https://twitter.com/brentblawat`

✦ Follow Marc Van Orsouw at `https://twitter.com/PowerShellGuy`

✦ Follow `PoshCode.org` at `https://twitter.com/PoshCode`

✦ For more open source information, follow Packt Publishing at `http://twitter.com/#!/packtopensource`

Thank you for buying
Instant Windows PowerShell 3.0 Windows Management Instrumentation Starter

About Packt Publishing

Packt, pronounced 'packed', published its first book "*Mastering phpMyAdmin for Effective MySQL Management*" in April 2004 and subsequently continued to specialize in publishing highly focused books on specific technologies and solutions.

Our books and publications share the experiences of your fellow IT professionals in adapting and customizing today's systems, applications, and frameworks. Our solution based books give you the knowledge and power to customize the software and technologies you're using to get the job done. Packt books are more specific and less general than the IT books you have seen in the past. Our unique business model allows us to bring you more focused information, giving you more of what you need to know, and less of what you don't.

Packt is a modern, yet unique publishing company, which focuses on producing quality, cutting-edge books for communities of developers, administrators, and newbies alike. For more information, please visit our website: www.packtpub.com.

Writing for Packt

We welcome all inquiries from people who are interested in authoring. Book proposals should be sent to author@packtpub.com. If your book idea is still at an early stage and you would like to discuss it first before writing a formal book proposal, contact us; one of our commissioning editors will get in touch with you.

We're not just looking for published authors; if you have strong technical skills but no writing experience, our experienced editors can help you develop a writing career, or simply get some additional reward for your expertise.

PUBLISHING

**Microsoft Windows
PowerShell 3.0 First Look**

A quick, succinct guide to the new and exciting features in
PowerShell 3.0

Adam Driscoll

[PACKT] enterprise

Microsoft Windows PowerShell 3.0 First Look

ISBN: 978-1-84968-644-0   Paperback: 200 pages

A quick, succinct guide to the new and exciting features in
PowerShell 3.0

1. Explore and experience the new features found in
    PowerShell 3.0

2. Understand the changes to the language and the
    reasons why they were implemented

3. Discover new cmdlets and modules available in
    Windows 8 and Server 8

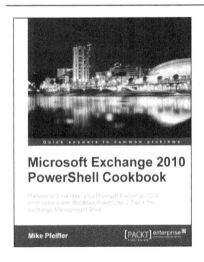

**Microsoft Exchange 2010
PowerShell Cookbook**

Manage and maintain your Microsoft Exchange 2010
environment with Windows PowerShell 2.0 and the
Exchange Management Shell

Mike Pfeiffer

[PACKT] enterprise

Microsoft Exchange 2010 PowerShell Cookbook

ISBN: 978-1-84968-246-6   Paperback: 480 pages

Manage and maintain your Microsoft Exchange 2010
environment with Windows PowerShell 2.0 and the
Exchange Management Shell

1. Step-by-step instructions on how to write scripts
    for nearly every aspect of Exchange 2010 including
    the Client Access Server, Mailbox, and Transport
    server roles

2. Understand the core concepts of Windows
    PowerShell 2.0 that will allow you to write
    sophisticated scripts and one-liners used with the
    Exchange Management Shell

3. Learn how to write scripts and functions, schedule
    scripts to run automatically, and generate complex
    reports

Please check **www.PacktPub.com** for information on our titles

SQL Server 2012 with PowerShell V3 Cookbook

SQL Server 2012 with PowerShell V3 Cookbook

ISBN: 978-1-84968-646-4   Paperback: 634 pages

Increase your productivity as a DBA, developer, or IT Pro, by using PowerShell with SQL Server to simplify database management and automate repetitive, mundane tasks.

1. Provides over a hundred practical recipes that utilize PowerShell to automate, integrate and simplify SQL Server tasks

2. Offers easy to follow, step-by-step guide to getting the most out of SQL Server and PowerShell

3. Covers numerous guidelines, tips, and explanations on how and when to use PowerShell cmdlets, WMI, SMO, .NET classes or other components

Windows Server 2012 Hyper-V Cookbook

Windows Server 2012 Hyper-V Cookbook

ISBN: 978-1-84968-442-2   Paperback: 304 pages

Over 50 simply but incredibly effective recipes for mastering the administration of Windows Server Hyper-V

1. Take advantage of numerous Hyper-V best practices for administrators

2. Get to grips with migrating virtual machines between servers and old Hyper-V versions, automating tasks with PowerShell, providing a High Availability and Disaster Recovery environment, and much more

3. A practical Cookbook bursting with essential recipes

Please check **www.PacktPub.com** for information on our titles

www.ingramcontent.com/pod-product-compliance
Lightning Source LLC
LaVergne TN
LVHW080104070326
832902LV00014B/2423